Building a creative blend of the old and the new

Freedom in worship

TIM LOMAX

First published in 2001 by
KEVIN MAYHEW LTD
Buxhall, Stowmarket
Suffolk IP14 3BW

9 8 7 6 5 4 3 2 1 0

ISBN 1 84003 734 2
Catalogue No. 1500425

Cover design by Jonathan Stroulger
Edited and typeset by Elisabeth Bates

Printed in Great Britain

Contents

Contents

Acknowledgements

Thank you to Kate and all others who support me.

About Tim Lomax . . .

His vision . . .

- To reflect the one who won his heart, to win the hearts of others.
- To present the gospel, strengthen discipleship and help lead genuine, accessible worship.
- To promote God's worth and word through music and song.
- To help build a twenty-first-century church.

Background . . .

Became a Christian at the age of 9. As a teenager, began to be involved in the music and worship of his local church. Studied music and teaching at the University of Derby before moving into full-time Christian work in 1995. Until 1999 he was music director/worship leader and Youth and Children's worker for his home church – St Andrew's and St Peter's, Weston Coyney, Stoke-on-Trent. Here, much experience was gained in planning and leading worship, mission work, all-age worship and the production of church services, not to mention multimedia youth events and schools work.

Now . . .

Tim and his wife Kate live in Nottingham. Kate is training for the ordained ministry at St John's Theological College. Tim now dedicates his time to music and worship under the name of his ministry – Lokate Music. He is also music co-ordinator for St John's College.

What does Tim do?

- Leads worship (solo or with the Lokate band).
- Composes worship songs.
- Creates contemporary forms of worship.
- Writes Bible-based liturgy.
- Provides worship workshops and training.
- Plans and leads all-age worship.
- Provides worship and music audits for forward-thinking churches.
- Provides teaching and lecturing on worship and music.

Web site: www.lokate-music.co.uk

Introduction

This book is designed as a user-friendly resource to help you deliver genuine worship that is creative and Spirit-impacted. Provided are a selection of ready-to-use contemporary service outlines blending the essential components of worship with the best of old and new features. These combine to initiate a flowing journey of praise, response and openness to God. Use them together with the concepts and techniques of the opening chapters to develop your worship, spark innovation or inject creativity.

Liturgy – making dry bones live

All church services make use of *liturgy*, the pattern and flow of worship. Many churches tend to use the formal liturgy of words to express worship. Other churches are less formal and employ a more open or spontaneous style of liturgy. However, there is a danger in both types of worship. It is common to find ourselves creating worship that is dictated by traditions, expectations, habits and set patterns as opposed to worship that is formed on the basis of what ought to be included – the essential ingredients. When this happens we find that our worship is lacking. For example, worship often includes little opportunity for personal expression, little expectancy for God to do a new thing and limited freedom for us to receive from God or express the wonderful gifts of the Spirit. In addition we often do little in response to hearing God's word.

It is important to see that by setting liturgy in a renewed, creative and open framework we can bring worship to life, making dry bones live. We need to stimulate more than the intellect by engaging the senses and the heart. Liturgy is only the framework for worship and it should be regarded as scaffolding, not a cage. It provides a wonderful foundation for us to express our heartfelt worship imaginatively.

By adding more than just the usual hymn/song slots, readings and talk to a liturgy, worship can be transformed. I believe that we can do more to encourage people to express themselves within worship. It can be beneficial to have a basic framework provided through formal or informal liturgy as it may help participants to worship in truth, focus attention on God and structure essential elements of Christian living such as forgiveness, prayer, belief, Communion and hearing the word of God. However, there is the danger that people may hide behind the liturgy, traditions and patterns of a church and go through the motions. That is why we must actively encourage individuals and churches to offer *themselves* within worship – their hearts, thoughts, gifts, experiences, desires, emotions, prayers and thanks. Such things are forever changing. God is Spirit and should be worshipped in a deeply personal way, from our spirit to God who is Spirit (John 4:24).

The Holy Spirit is creative and life giving – he fills our worship bringing growth, development and constant renewal to the church. That is why we need to provide space for the Spirit to move and act within liturgy. Thus, we will allow worship to become a two-way act of communication in which we give to God and expect to receive from him. To put it simply, we will desire the Spirit as well as the truth. To realise this desire we must try to ensure that within all our services we are open to the Holy Spirit and desire to see him impact every aspect of worship.

Essential ingredients

When included and expressed within a liturgy framework the following components can help build genuine worship that is creative and Spirit impacted:

- A desire to see the Spirit of God impacting worship
- Praise
- Adoration
- Intimacy
- Reflection
- Silence
- Response to God's word
- Extended times of open worship
- Intercession
- Prayer ministry
- Freedom of expression
- Creativity

Note – Holy Communion (the sharing of bread and wine) is also an essential component of worship but it is not celebrated in every service.

The type of worship highlighted in this book aims to provide opportunities for Spirit impacted worship by including the above components within a creative liturgy framework. Ideas such as background music, visual elements, practical responses/rituals, quiet reflection and creative forms of prayer then help bring the worship to life by stimulating other senses as well as the heart.

Obviously, we have to guard against the 'recipe mentality' which plagues liturgy at the best of times. We can all too easily presume that by including ingredients *x*, *y* and *z* the desired outcome will be realised. We should be mindful of this and remind ourselves that we are providing opportunities within worship, seeking to provide ways in which we encounter God and ways in which God encounters us. By doing this we will help lead individuals and churches on their Spiritual journey of growth so that within every service they are given the opportunity to worship with all their heart and depart changed, renewed, encouraged, healed or challenged, and, God willing, filled with his Spirit!

Why use this book?

You may be thinking that you have lots of truth and not enough Spirit and creativity within your church worship. Perhaps you wish to do things in a fresh way whilst still blending the old with the new. Maybe you have a heart to facilitate innovative worship but lack the ideas, vision and time. Perhaps you have identified spiritual needs in your congregation that can be met through the introduction of this type of worship. Alternatively, you may wish to broaden your horizons and experiences as a leader of services or worship leader. This book has two major parts; it contains ready-to-use plans, guidelines and ideas for blending effective contemporary worship plus the concepts needed to develop worship that is increasingly open to the power of God.

How do I use this book?

As a resource. It could act as a catalyst in the life of the church or in your own ministry. It provides you with the material for effective worship and the ready-made service plans for you to introduce into your church. The church worship can then begin to develop as you enhance your worship-planning and -leading skills. All the plans and ideas in this book are not set in stone, they are there to spark life. So, feel free to use them, adapt them and then invent your own! All hymn and song suggestions are taken from *The Source*, *The Source 2*, *Release* and *Sing Glory*, which are available from your local Christian bookshop or Kevin Mayhew Publishers.

Each worship pattern provides a detailed plan. Most follow a theme that can easily be adapted to fit particular readings of your choice, special events and times of change within your church. Each plan is accompanied with full instructions to guide you and your colleagues through the worship, song/hymn suggestions, prayers, responses/rituals and other creative ideas. These can be followed or adapted to suit your own situation or style. Further creative elements such as dance, signing (as used for the deaf), drama, visual ideas and responses/rituals can easily be added to each plan where appropriate along with other suitable ideas or traditions you may have. (For details on creative ideas see **creativity** within 'The essential components of creative Spirit-impacted worship', page 19.)

User-friendly and innovative worship? – making the most of new technology

All worship should be user-friendly and accessible to leaders and congregation. This means that we should do our utmost to make people at ease with the liturgy we use by making it simple to follow with any printed words easy to find and read. Similarly, leaders of worship should be clear about the outline and flow of worship.

At the beginning of the twenty-first century we have so much opportunity to make worship ever more user-friendly and innovative. By employing the technology on offer we can ensure that printed elements of liturgy or hymn and song words are readily accessible. This can be done by projecting all words onto screens or by producing weekly service sheets. In addition, images and video material can easily be projected onto screens opening up many more opportunities. We can use overhead projectors that make use of printed acetate sheets or in some cases use video/data projectors that process computer-generated texts, images and video material. Personal computer software also makes it possible to create professional standard service sheets for use within worship. Obviously this goes against the traditional book culture that dominates many churches. However, the experience of some churches has found that it is this culture that can help make church-going an off-putting experience. Visitors and young people in particular are expected to wade through unfamiliar books often shifting from page to page or even from one book to another! This needn't be the case. There is so much potential for us to make church worship a user-friendly experience; all it takes is a little preparation and courage. The benefits are numerous. Firstly, you may find that you save money this way by spending less on projection or printed service sheets than you would on books. Secondly, you can be more creative and flexible by introducing alternative prayers, images, artwork and layouts appropriate to your particular church or community. Finally, the selection of hymns and songs becomes much freer when you are not tied to those included in the books you use. New songs can be introduced whenever you like (with proper copyright). Needless to say you may have to overcome some difficulties but don't lose heart. Modern technology is not essential to innovative worship – it only helps. Use the ideas and concepts contained in this book to develop what you already do. If you have a heart for creative God-filled worship then you will be able to achieve great things.

Combining the best of the old and the new

Worship that effectively combines the best of both the old and new will strike a healthy balance between material brought with us from the past and contemporary components which will help take the church into the future.

The best of the old

Genuine worship makes use of the best from the old – traditions, hymns, songs and written liturgies. This way services are built upon the wonderful expressions of worship that have gone before us. Often timeless truths are wrapped up in beautiful resources of faith that shine just as brilliantly now as they did in years gone by. Traditional hymns often encapsulate sentiments and meaning that we would otherwise struggle to communicate. Some expressions of faith have been passed down from the Early Church in the first centuries AD and many of these are contained within written prayers still used by many churches (e.g. the Anglican Church). Written liturgies (formal worship patterns) have also evolved over the centuries and they include many meaningful traditions that engage the heart and express faith practically.

It is important to remember that none of the above elements of worship carry merit merely for being old and established within the Church. They should be included in services for one reason only – because they are an effective medium for offering praise to God. Now, this reason is open to debate, as you have probably found in your own church! Worship must be relevant in order for it to be offered genuinely to God. We cannot worship the Lord fully if we do not understand what we are communicating or if we cannot relate to the style in which it is being communicated. One of the many beauties of worship is that it can express timeless truths to and of God in a contemporary manner. We can connect with and make use of the everyday things of the age in which we live to create worship that is relevant and meaningful. If we neglect this, worship can appear out of date, out of touch and irrelevant even though it may be packed full of truths and profound expressions of faith. We ought to remember that many people are used to pop music, computer games, the internet and video. Almost all of us experience multimedia sound- and sight-bites. Therefore, we can adapt church worship so that it connects with the life experiences of most people. When planning worship ask yourself the question – would most people (not church people) connect with this hymn, prayer and tradition or the style in which it is done? We should try to ensure then that worship is not only glorifying to God but also accessible and user-friendly for all. If someone walked into your church off the street would they easily pick up on all that was going on? This question is well worth consideration.

This means that planners of worship ought to select from the best of the 'old' resources available (hymns, traditions, formal liturgies and prayers). Obviously opinions and tastes differ so here are a few criteria to consider:

- Traditions (e.g. rituals) included within worship should be meaningful for *all* people present, should engage the heart and glorify God alone.
- Hymns ought to be user-friendly (easy to sing and understand), versatile (suitable for contemporary musical arrangements) and attractive to the congregation.

- Prayers should also be user-friendly (easy to read and understand) and suitable for creative ideas to be added (e.g. visual elements).

One of the most effective ways to employ the best of the 'old' material is to give it a contemporary flavour. Traditional elements are then more likely to connect with the congregation. There are various ways to do this. Here are some ideas:

- Include traditional elements within a mainly contemporary framework that includes innovative material and ideas.
- Arrange hymns in a contemporary style (e.g. music group, band or piano arrangements – a drum or percussion rhythm can help).
- Combine traditional elements (e.g. confession, written prayers and rituals) with contemporary background music (live or recorded).
- Include innovative visual ideas (signing, dance, symbols, art, photographs, video material, computer-generated images) alongside traditional elements.

The best of the new

Genuine worship also employs the best of the new, 'here and now' elements that help make our services contemporary, relevant and meaningful today – new songs, prayers, creative ideas, modern music and new technology. Such resources help to ensure that: a. worshippers relate to all the content and participate fully; b. all components of worship are easily accessible to everyone; c. worship is user-friendly; d. worship is a stimulating and inspirational encounter with God; and e. worship is creative and continually refreshed.

The last of these points I believe is the most crucial if we are to build worship that includes the best of the new. For this to happen we should set out to be creative and desire our worship to be constantly updated. God is creative and his Spirit brings creativity so that we in turn are free to express our faith and praises in imaginative, experiential ways – see **creativity** from 'The essential components of creative Spirit-impacted worship', page 19, for details of this.

When we seek to create worship using the best of the new we will find that we are actually building towards the future instead of holding on to the past. As God's people we should be looking to move forwards, asking God to do a new thing within his church. When we employ innovative material, resources, styles and ideas we demonstrate our passion for moving on looking to the church of tomorrow.

So, how do you select from the best of the new? Here are some suggestions to help:

- Only choose material that you think is sound. Unlike traditional material new ideas and resources have not stood the test of time so if in doubt leave it out.
- New material and ideas should be meaningful and accessible for *all* people present, should engage the heart and glorify God alone.
- All new material should be user-friendly and easy to engage with.
- New material should help create a worshipful environment in which we encounter God. If it does not help to achieve this goal then it is not worth having.
- Include new material because of spiritual benefits, not to be 'modern'.

The essential components of creative Spirit-impacted worship

In order to make use of the service outlines in this book and develop creative Spirit-impacted worship it is important to understand the concepts and components on which they are built.

It is my belief that all worship should be continually creative and God-filled. These attributes go together and you will find that where the Spirit is there will also be creativity. It is important for the church to realise that such attributes are not a matter of taste and that they should not accompany one particular style of worship only. They must be seen as essential to all worship. If we are to meet the spiritual needs of growing Christians we must expose them to worship containing these attributes.

The components discussed below can help build worship that is creative and Spirit impacted. By incorporating them in your services you will discover worship that can be refreshed week after week, creative both in planning and spontaneity and open to the Spirit of God. The ready-to-use Service Outlines contained in this book are built with these components in mind.

A desire to see the Spirit of God impacting worship

And with that he breathed on them and said, 'Receive the Holy Spirit . . .' (John 20:22)

True worship expresses our relationship with God. We communicate our praise, thanks, adoration and prayers. We express what we believe, our repentance and commitment and we respond to God's word. A worship liturgy can wonderfully encapsulate all of these things and yet to leave it at this would mean that we miss out on the full picture and the complete relationship with God. As part of our life and relationship with him he has promised to be with us and in us by the power of his Holy Spirit so that he is ever present in our lives, our church and our worship. This dimension of worship goes beyond words. God desires to make himself known and his presence felt but he also longs to fill us with his breath of life so that we can live and worship in Spirit and truth thus expressing and demonstrating spiritual gifts and fruit in order that we may give him glory. Without openness to the Holy Spirit and a desire to see him active (inspiring our understanding of the word, bringing personal growth and renewal, healing, empowering us with gifts of the Spirit) worship falls short of the wonderful kingdom experience God intends it to be. We can make Spirit-impacted worship our heart's desire and pray earnestly for God to move amongst us in power. Much of our worship already expresses this desire. Many of our prayers and traditions acknowledge the presence of God's Spirit and our need of him. However, we can also express our desire for the Holy Spirit through other points within services; for example, times of sung worship, silence or reflection.

Praise

Praise the Lord. How good it is to sing praises to our God, how pleasant and fitting to praise him! (Psalm 147:1)

When we gather together as congregations to praise Almighty God we join with all of heaven and earth. There is nothing greater than praising the Lord – as the psalmist says it is good and fitting. When we truly know God we naturally desire to praise him (for his character, his love, his promises, his blessings, all that he has done and all that he is going to do). A praising church is an advancing people using praise as a powerful weapon in spiritual warfare, a growing people advancing in mission declaring praise inside and outside the church and a rejoicing people who enjoy God. So then we should encourage each other in this pursuit and allow ourselves to express freely and gladly our heartfelt thanks and praise. Why not focus times of praise at the beginning or end of services specifically on God's character or our Saviour Jesus Christ, the blessings we enjoy or our thanks for all that he has done in our lives? Alternatively, use praise and proclamation to conclude a service so that you leave having declared God's might and victory.

Adoration

On coming to the house, they saw the child with his mother Mary, and they bowed down and worshipped him. Then they opened their treasures and presented him with gifts . . . (Matthew 2:11)

The underlying aim of all services is to worship God, to give him his worth ('worth-ship'). Adoration is defined as the act of worshipping. When we draw close to God and stay in his presence our desire is to adore him, expressing our intense admiration and offering our deep love for him. The Magi on seeing the Son of God in the form of a new-born baby bowed down and worshipped him. Today we now enjoy the opportunity to come into the house (the church building) and draw close to God through our *risen* Lord Jesus Christ. However, our response can be the same as that of the Magi. Within all services there should be the opportunity for us to bow down and worship our Lord. We need the space to open our own treasures and offer our gifts. Times of worship should enable us as Christians to declare our adoration of God and continually offer ourselves (all that we are and have) as living sacrifices. Again written liturgy provides an excellent framework for us to do this. We have access to words that express these sentiments wonderfully. However, we must allow people to express worship personally as well as corporately, spontaneously as the Magi did as well as with prepared words. We need to use liturgy effectively in order to lead people on a journey into the presence of their Saviour and provide them with space and time to dwell there. Sung worship and music can provide the environment for this to happen. We need to ensure that we use with sensitivity songs and hymns that express our adoration and combine them with written prayers imaginatively. Worship should flow naturally and we need to use liturgy to its full potential so that at an appropriate point we move from praise into adoration (see also **extended times of open worship**, page 16).

Intimacy

When a woman who had lived a sinful life in that town learned that Jesus was eating at the Pharisee's house, she brought an alabaster jar of perfume, and she stood behind him at his feet weeping, she began to wet his feet with her tears.

Then she wiped them with her hair, kissed them and poured perfume on them. (Luke 7:37-38)

Having drawn close enough to bow at the feet of the Lord and adore him we are now close enough to kiss him. In his presence we are aware not only of our sinfulness but also our forgiveness. Jesus has given us so much, his love for us is vast and we are overcome with gratitude and admiration. Our response – to love him unreservedly and to enjoy the intimate relationship he encourages. It is then that we are more aware of our feelings for him (love, gratitude, loyalty) and his closeness to us (his love in our hearts, understanding and warm regard). Just like the sinful woman we are at liberty to express our heart personally, freely, emotionally, despite what others think and regardless of cultural taboos. Similarly our worship becomes a fragrant offering to our Lord. Intimacy is an aspect of our relationship with God that we should openly encourage within services and times of worship. Through it our relationship deepens and we grow in the love of our heavenly Father through Jesus Christ.

Intimacy is something that can be allowed for within a worship flow contained within a liturgy. Teaching on this component of worship is invaluable and in this way you can encourage your congregation to seek it. Times of sung worship also provide opportunity for us to enjoy it. By using songs that express aspects of our relationship with God and allowing space for people to rest in his presence whilst sensitive worship music plays in the background we will have the opportunity to enjoy the intimacy which we long for.

Reflection

May the words of my mouth and the meditation of my heart be pleasing in your sight . . . (Psalm 19:14)

Have you ever left a church service feeling that you were never given the opportunity to catch your breath, respond to God on a personal level or give him what was in your heart at the time? You read printed words, heard the minister speaking on behalf of the congregation or looked on as the worship leader filled every available space with singing and you left feeling that you were spoken for and were not allowed to express *your* faith using *your* own words or thoughts in *your* own way. I'm sure that many of us have encountered this. Unfortunately, it is rare to see space for personal or corporate reflection included within liturgy. And yet it has such an important role to play in our spiritual lives. Worship should include time for us to think, meditate, listen and ponder within God's presence. This can be done by introducing space or time within open worship for people to use how they wish (to think upon God's character or his love, to meditate on his word or as the hymn expresses so beautifully to 'ponder anew what the Almighty can do'). Why not try using sensitive background music after a time of sung worship, and silence between readings or after the talk. Alternatively, try to stimulate reflection by using drama, video clips, images, meditations or even songs to listen to.

Silence

But the Lord is in his holy temple; let all the earth be silent before him. (Habakkuk 2:20)

God makes his presence known to us within our place of worship. The simple response to his glory in our midst is reverent silence. Not because we show reverence by being silent but because when we truly know that we are in the presence of Almighty God we are lost for words and want to stay there still and quiet. However, silence before God is constantly neglected within worship. I don't know whether we are afraid of silence but as a rule we tend to shy away from it, filling it as soon as possible. If only we could rediscover the value of silence within our worship we would have more to offer people who doubtless lead busy lives and crave to have their souls restored by quiet waters. Silence is such an easy component to include within worship whether it is planned or unplanned. Why not leave space for silence after a time of sung worship, during the prayer time or at the beginning/end of Communion (the sharing of bread and wine). By including silence you will also have the opportunity to encourage your congregation to listen to God and be open to receive gifts of the Spirit that can be expressed afterwards (e.g. prophecy, tongues).

Response to God's word

Do not merely listen to the word . . . (James 1:22)

God's word requires a response. We should be listeners and doers. This means that after a talk or sermon we can give space for a response process to start (e.g. commitment, repentance, healing, forgiveness). Perhaps a time of sung worship with response in mind, a period of quiet for people to begin reflecting on how they can act on what they have just heard or a time of corporate prayer and ministry.

We can be imaginative when responding to God because we don't have to use words. That is why visual and practical responses or rituals can be a wonderful aid. They allow people to demonstrate what their heart is feeling and make a public or private response. Whatever the method, it is vitally important that we do our utmost to introduce response within worship. By doing this the seeds of God's word are given the opportunity to be watered by the Spirit. Individuals and churches are free to start exploring what God's word means for them, to commit themselves to it and store it in their hearts as well as their minds. It is important, however, to be reminded of how crucial it is for the talk to prompt a response. If a talk is based on theory only, passing information on as in an academic lecture, then the word given will most probably prompt an intellectual response (or blank faces!). However, if the talk challenges the heart too then it is more likely to prompt a heartfelt response.

Extended times of open worship

To put it simply, worship is a journey in which we travel towards God, offer ourselves in praise and adoration, receive from him and then move on with him, re-focused, re-committed, renewed and changed. Extended times of open sung worship can help us move on this journey. Worship can flow naturally from one component to another (see example below) simply by using appropriate songs and hymns. Instrumental music (played by music group, band or organ) can link songs and provide the backdrop for open worship in which people are encouraged to express worship freely. Praise, prayers, testimonies, and in some churches spiritual gifts including prophecies, singing in the Spirit, speaking in tongues (accompanied with interpretation) or words of knowledge can be shared. Specific opportunity for this can be provided in 'open time' (as in the worship plans provided). Alternatively, people can simply be still and reflective. Worship leaders can help direct these times by encouraging an appropriate response, focus or flow but what should be prevalent is an overall openness to the Holy Spirit.

Example:

Call to worship → Praise → Adoration → Intimacy → Reflection/Stillness

Any liturgy (formal or informal) can incorporate times of extended worship perfectly. Many liturgies begin by calling us to worship and focus our attention on praising God. An extended time of worship would flow naturally from this. Other aspects of the liturgy and pattern could then be included, such as a time of confession. Alternatively an extended time of open worship could follow the talk and incorporate response, prayer or prayer ministry.

Some points to remember about extended times of worship –

- They can follow a worship flow or part of one (see 'Planning worship', page 29).
- The music should be led well and sensitively by the music group, worship band or organist (linking songs, providing beautiful background or instrumental music, worshipping through the playing of the music and touching people's hearts).
- To lead extended times of open worship you ought to be familiar and comfortable with them. You should expect the Holy Spirit to impact the worship!
- The congregation should also be encouraged to worship freely and be open to the Holy Spirit.
- Be prepared for the Holy Spirit to move in sovereign power.

Intercession

Traditionally prayers are said by one person on behalf of others. However, if these prayers are to be truly 'of the people' we ought to include a little more freedom within the intercession liturgy so that members of the congregation can offer their own prayers. Space or silence in between sections of the prayers are ideal ways of engaging others either silently or out loud. We can also be creative with prayer and use more than spoken words. Subject headings on overhead or data projectors can prompt the prayers of the congregation, so too can newspaper headlines, photographs and video material. Background music either played live by the organ/music group or recorded music can help create a prayerful atmosphere. By using simple ideas imaginatively intercession can encapsulate more effectively the prayers we wish to offer to God at the time and become more relevant to the congregation offering them.

Prayer ministry

And pray in the Spirit on all occasions with all kinds of prayers and requests. (Ephesians 6:18)

In my view all main times of church worship should include opportunity for prayer ministry. It is one of the ways in which a church looks after the spiritual and physical welfare of its members. By making it available at appropriate times within the service people have the chance to ask for prayer and make their requests to God with the help of others. It also means that they can deal with issues highlighted during the worship. In addition, churches can pray for those with specific ministries or those who are about to embark on them. When done thoroughly and effectively prayer ministry becomes an essential part of church family life. It is vital to note the value of guidelines, training and team meetings for this ministry and also the need to establish a framework for logistics (where will the prayer take place? when? will music continue? etc.).

Freedom of expression

Now the Lord is the Spirit, and where the Spirit of the Lord is, there is freedom. (2 Corinthians 3:17)

The Holy Spirit releases us in worship to express our hearts unreservedly. He enables us to worship with our whole being – body, mind and spirit. The Bible is littered with examples of how we can express worship. The important thing to remember is that in addition to the usual elements of worship contained within liturgy we actively encourage people to enjoy the freedom of expression that the Holy Spirit brings so that they worship fully and share gifts of the Spirit.

We can provide people with space for spontaneous expression (aloud or privately). This can be to say prayers, truths about God, testimony, proclaiming victory, praising God's goodness, thanking him or lamenting. Shouting is also a way in which we can express triumph, joy and victory. Opportunity for this type of expression can come at numerous points within a service. Probably the most natural place would be within open times of extended worship.

Expressing worship with our whole body is a good thing. Movement can capture emotion, enhance and even visualise our offering or response to God:

- Dancing is a wonderful form of physical expression. It is a sign of overflowing joy. Psalm 149:3 says 'Let them praise his name with dancing . . .'
- Clapping is something we are used to doing but not necessarily within worship. Just as we can applaud each other we can also applaud the Lord. Psalm 47:1 says 'Clap your hands, all you nations; shout to God with cries of joy.'
- Raising hands – 'Lift up your hands in the sanctuary and praise the Lord' (Psalm 134:2). The use of our hands can be a very expressive form of body language. To lift our hands in praise and prayer is a very clear indication of looking upwards and God-wards.
- Bowing or kneeling – 'Come, let us bow down in worship, let us kneel before the Lord our Maker; for he is our God . . .' (Psalm 95:6-7). We humble ourselves in complete reverence 'for he is our God' almighty and awesome.

These forms of expression can be encouraged throughout times of worship. It must be stressed that they should not be done for tradition or for any other reason than to glorify God. They demonstrate how we feel towards him and if hearts are not engaged they are empty gestures.

The Holy Spirit also empowers Christians to express gifts of the Spirit. These include prophecy, speaking in tongues, interpretation, words of knowledge and healing. These gifts are given for the common good. Everyone does not receive the same gifts so this provides wonderful diversity and variety within the church. We should welcome gifts of the Spirit particularly within services and allow them to shape and inspire our worship, church life and ministries. God makes himself known through his gifts and we should always be willing for him to do so. Open times of extended worship can help provide the space and the environment for spiritual gifts to be shared.

By providing biblical teaching and leading by example we can encourage congregations to express themselves in the Spirit. As leaders and planners of worship it is our responsibility to provide worship environments that openly encourage freedom of expression.

Creativity

The Holy Spirit is creative and seeks to bring creativity to worship. He blesses our skills and talents. He inspires and even sets ideas and aspects of worship ablaze all for the benefit of the church and to bring glory to the Trinity. Creativity brings relevance and dynamism to each church in its local setting so it is something we should desire to see and facilitate in worship as much as possible.

Singing new songs is something we should actively encourage. Not only is it biblical, it is also a great way to renew and refresh worship. Often new songs capture a moment in church life or spark new life. Keep a lookout for new music resources or subscribe to a good publication of new material such as those available from world wide worship (see address below). You may well discover someone in your own church with a gift for songwriting. If this is the case then help them to develop this gift by providing training or a mentor. It is important for good home-grown songs to be used and made more widely available so include them in your worship and submit them (simple score + demo tape) to a publishing company. World wide worship are always on the lookout for new songs:

Praise & Worship Manager
WWW
Buxhall
Stowmarket
Suffolk
IP14 3BW

When we are open to the creativity of the Holy Spirit within liturgy we may experience *music in the Spirit*. Obviously, the Spirit is present in all worship but sometimes he touches us very specifically causing us to respond spontaneously through music. Musicians can *play in the Spirit* creating new music and a beautiful environment in which we enjoy the presence of God – listening to him, perhaps speaking in tongues or just resting. At other times *singing in the Spirit* may spring from a time of worship. This is the spontaneous singing of a new song to the Lord. It may include the singing of tongues or more usual words of worship sung simply. It can come from an existing song and can move back into a song afterwards. It is not exclusive to musicians or worship leaders – it's for everyone. *Prophetic song* is something entirely different. It is a word from the Bible or direct from God which is sung by an individual instead of spoken. *Prayer song* can be spontaneous or pre-written. It is simply the singing of prayers. Some existing songs can act as a prayer of the people. At other times there can be sung responses to spoken prayers. Similarly to singing in the Spirit, Prayer song can spring from a time of sung worship as people are inspired to sing out their prayers spontaneously.

One thing is clear, we need to be *imaginative* if worship is to be creative. Today through the media and modern technology we are bombarded with amazing sound- and sight-bites. When a worship environment is built almost entirely on a collection of words (no matter how profound they are) it seems so poor in comparison to the stimulating experiences we receive in many other places. This is not to say that we should merely seek an 'experience' through worship but that God has given us such stimulating tools to use creatively within worship. By using these we can form liturgy imaginatively. To help increase creativity in worship you could use talented people from within your congregation. They don't necessarily have to be professional, just gifted, called and good enough to serve the church well. Don't worry if you don't have an array of creative people within your congregation. It doesn't mean that you are not open to creativity, just that you lack the people power.

Creative ideas to help stimulate the mind, heart and senses in worship

Music

- Combining liturgy with music. Music and spoken worship moving in an unbroken flow as in the Service Outlines provided. Musicians need to improvise sensitively and link songs with instrumental sections. Can provide a natural and beautiful worship environment.
- Background music to prayer, readings, meditations and reflections, visual elements, dance or mime. Requires improvised or recorded music to create the appropriate atmosphere.
- Songs to minister (live or recorded). Used at appropriate times within worship to encourage, convey a message, highlight a theme or lead to a point of response.

Visual elements

- Computer-generated images
- Art
- Video material
- Symbols
- Displays
- Banners
- Flags
- Stained-glass windows
- Icons
- Candles

Practical responses/rituals

Visual and practical ways in which people respond to God, for example:

- Committing yourself to Christ by placing your thumb-print on a white cross (see 'Repent, believe and follow' Service Outline)
- Believer's baptism by immersion

Drama

- Sketches
- Mime
- Musicals
- Monologues
- Dramatised Bible readings

Meditation

- Looking at inspiring images, symbols or icons
- Imagination journeys or stories
- Written reflections

Movement

- Dance
- Signing (using sign language can not only help those who are deaf but also brings expression to worship)

Creative prayer

- Using images to inspire prayer
- Using video material to spark prayer
- Using newspaper cuttings (on OHP) to lead prayer
- Incorporating silence for personal prayer
- Incorporating space for prayers offered aloud
- Group prayer

Setting

- Seating
- Layout
- An environment of visual impact

Taste, touch and smell

- Incense
- Fragrant oils
- Meaningful objects to hold (e.g. scented petals, palm crosses)
- Bread and wine
- Bitter herbs (from a Passover meal)

Good practice

All of us should strive to implement and maintain good practice within worship. Every church regardless of size, wealth, resources and personnel can work towards aims and goals within a structure of clear guidelines. Worship is the prime reason for a church's existence and those involved in the planning and leading of it need to know in which way they are headed and how to arrive there together. Good practice is a tremendous asset to any church. It can be the catalyst to spark effective ministry, it can create continuity within church life and best of all it can be passed on. Here are some aspects that help create good practice:

A vision that is shared

As part of every overall church vision there can be a specific vision for worship; how it will develop in the future, the spiritual needs to be met, the attributes it will contain, the beliefs it will be built on and how it will relate to the rest of church life. It is important that we do consider a vision for worship so that it is allowed to move and grow, incorporating the everyday things, new resources, effective ideas and, most importantly, what God is doing within each church. The vision, however, must be drawn up collectively and shared by the whole church. This may involve in-depth discussions, prayer and teaching.

Training

Training is vital to the implementation of good practice. It enables those involved in the planning, leading or supporting of worship to develop their gifts, skills and spirituality. If we are to enable church members to have effective ministries in the area of worship then we must be prepared where possible to provide them with appropriate training. We are not just talking about worship leaders, preachers or musicians. We must also equip others who play a part in services – those who lead the prayers, the prayer ministry team, drama team, dancers, signers, the welcome team, PA operators, etc. Why not find out what training is available in your area or seek out gifted people from your own congregation who may do in-house training? Alternatively, be on the lookout for conferences run by other churches or organisations (e.g. www.lokate-music.co.uk).

Teamwork

This is a very biblical practice and can be put to very effective use within the area of worship. Often responsibilities in worship are shared but rarely co-ordinated. Each person does his or her thing in isolation to everything and everyone else. For example, often the person who chooses the songs and hymns does so without linking up with the people who will actually lead the service or preach. Now there is no doubt that God can still operate in such circumstances but it is certainly better to plan thoroughly looking at the whole picture before focusing in on details such as songs. For this to happen teamwork is a must. One idea would be to create a worship-planning group responsible for the overall co-ordination. This would be made up by worship leaders, readers, music group leader/organist and group leaders for prayer ministry team, drama group, dance group, etc. They could meet to pray and discuss forthcoming services – responsibilities, content, themes, preachers, creative ideas and so on. All those involved would immediately have an impression of what will go on and would then be able to prepare in advance. The worship leader for each service would then have co-ordinating and delegating responsibility for details such as service plan, songs/hymns, etc. This way all responsibility does not rest on one person (i.e. the vicar or pastor). By combining gifts worship benefits from collective planning.

Prayer

Prayer is an essential ingredient to worship and should be done in the planning and thinking stages, at any practices and before the actual service. Through prayer we communicate our need of God's inspiration and his Holy Spirit, our longing to see his will done and our desire to hear him speak to us. By praying at every turn from start to finish we give our gifts, ideas and plans to God for him to alter or confirm and then bless and use for his glory. Prayer for our worship should involve all those concerned. If teams of people share the responsibility of planning they should also share the responsibility for prayer.

Music

Music is one of the key elements to a service and can help or hinder worship. That is why its role is so crucial. Many church leaders have said that some of the most important church ministry appointments are the worship leaders, musical director and musicians. Music is a God-given part of worship. It can set the tone, help create a worshipful environment and give voice to our hearts. It is not sufficient to hold to the attitude that music simply accompanies singing and that all you need is any old set of accompanists. If someone can speak we don't automatically ask them to preach and so if someone can play an instrument this does not automatically mean that they are suitable to help lead worship. There are other factors to consider – calling, gifting, heart and commitment. Obviously levels of ability vary from person to person and from church to church but if we take music as seriously as we should then we can work on a vision that encourages, trains and equips the dedicated people who play week after week. Often smaller churches struggle to find gifted musicians. This can cause some difficulties and often people who are unsure of their ability end up helping out. The important thing to remember is that all churches should develop the ministries of their musicians. If someone has the potential to improve and play music effectively within worship then it is the responsibility of church leaders to help him/her realise this potential. Some churches find that they have no one to provide music within services. Although this is not ideal it is not a disaster either and unaccompanied singing or pre-recorded backing tracks such as midi song files as provided by DM Music (www.dm-music.co.uk) can provide a suitable alternative to live instruments.

The music used in a service should make use of the best of the old and the new. It must also connect with the congregation with regard to age or social background, reflect the diversity of taste, be theologically sound (if in doubt leave it out) and be appropriate to the mode of accompaniment (i.e. guitar, piano, organ, band). New songs should also be introduced regularly (it's biblical!).

A great technique for song and hymn management is a play list. This is the complete list of hymns and songs appropriate for each church over a whole year. It can contain anything from 70-100 songs/hymns selected by a worship-planning group in consultation with the music group, organist, etc. The play list is reviewed every 12 months so that material no longer needed may be omitted and new material included. When the new songs and hymns have been chosen you could hold a new songs praise evening for the church. In time the songs on the list become very familiar enabling the congregation to participate confidently. A theme index can be drawn up for the list and OHP acetates can be made for all songs/hymns.

Obtaining copyright is a necessity if you are to reproduce any printed music or words to songs or hymns. The simplest way to do this is by purchasing a Christian Copyright Licence (address shown below).

Christian Copyright Licensing (Europe) Ltd
Chantry House
22 Upperton Road
Eastbourne
East Sussex
BN21 1BF

Good resources are needed if church music is to be effective, drawing on the best of the old and the new. Ideally a church needs one good book to use as its basis for music (e.g. *The Source* – Kevin Mayhew). Then as new material becomes available (e.g. a series such as *Global Worship* – world wide worship, Kevin Mayhew) this can be added to existing resources. You don't have to buy duplicate copies of books either, just enough for all those concerned to have access to them (music group and worship leaders). By purchasing a copyright licence you can then photocopy enough music for the musicians and singers. The photocopied music can be stored in files and used much more easily on music stands.

For the latest information regarding music resources visit:
www.kevinmayhewltd.com

Getting the best out of a music group or worship band

This is something many churches struggle with. Often church leaders (who perhaps have little knowledge of music) are expected to establish a music group or oversee it. By including the following good practice guidelines more churches can hopefully be equipped with the knowledge they need to develop strong music groups.

The ideal make-up of the group

- Lead instrument (keyboard or guitar). To play the main part in the music.
- Lead singer. To lead the congregation in singing the melody and call any instructions during a song.
- Support instrument (guitar or keyboard). To accompany the main instrument.
- Support/harmony singers (one or two). To accompany the lead singer with harmonies or to take over the tune at a given point in a song.
- Bass guitar. To accompany the drum rhythm.

- Percussion. To add sensitive rhythm.
- Acoustic instruments (one or two). To add extra harmonies or to play the tune for introductions, endings and instrumentals.

For services that incorporate extended times of open worship the music leader (who is the lead singer and possibly plays the lead instrument) can be encouraged to become the worship leader. They will not necessarily lead the whole service but certainly the aspects of worship involving music and singing. The person who fulfils this role should be gifted, trained, appointed by the church, be a team player, have a servant heart and a clear sense of God's calling.

How should the group play together? – simple is best

- With microphones you really only need one singer or instrument to pick out the melody at any one time.
- The group should be encouraged to improvise and be creative in their music. If they struggle encourage them to get some training or to use *The Source* instrument scores available from Kevin Mayhew.
- The group should be encouraged to play from chords given in a song. This will enable them to improvise more readily and become more musically versatile. Again seek training if required.

Qualities and attitudes to encourage

- Worship, not performance; ensemble, not virtuoso solo.
- Everyone has equal status and is valued for their contribution.
- Servants of God and the church (accountability).
- The group should work hard to improve and set a high standard.
- Anyone involved in church music should have a clear calling and gift. They should be appointed by the church.
- Discipline is important. The group will need to be thorough, well rehearsed and prepared. Commitment, spiritual growth and maturity should be expected for such an important ministry.

Practices/rehearsals

- Should be times of worship and fellowship.
- There usually needs to be one main practice (approximately two hours if possible) plus warm-up and sound check before main worship (approximately 45 minutes where possible). Suggested outline:

  Drink and a chat
  Prayer
  Look at forthcoming service plans and what is required
  Immediate material (forthcoming week)
  Future material
  New material
  Prayer
- Plan worship thoroughly in consultation with the group and leader.

Position the music group well

This issue causes no end of problems in a church (within congregation and music group). However, there are several things to remember:

- The group should be seen (so that they can see the congregation and lead by example).
- The group should have sufficient space.
- Generally speaking the group need to be situated behind the PA speakers (to prevent feedback). You may need to reorder the church to find space. (This is a big issue but may be a real long-term advantage).

Encourage the group

- The church leader should get to know the members of the group (socially and at practices). He/she can be their adviser and meet with them regularly – to discuss forthcoming services and events, plan, pray and discuss a vision for the music and worship.
- The musicians should have the opportunity and freedom to express and develop their gifts.
- The group should be protected from unnecessary criticism.
- Gifted group leaders can be encouraged to lead worship, plan and select material. They should also be a member of the church council.
- Try to ensure that there is a good standard of sound equipment, operation and support available whenever the music group play.
- If you have a choir as well as a music group then it is important to build good relations. Help both groups to feel valued and needed. Set out clear guidelines as to what is expected of each group. Involve them both in the drawing up of your church vision for worship and show how each can help work towards it.

Getting the best out of the organist and choir

As organs and choirs are established aspects of many churches I'm sure you all know how to get the most out of them or to at least try! You will most probably have discovered that relationships are the key to either avoiding conflict or overcoming it!

Additional creative elements

Although music is the main creative element of a service other elements (such as drama and signing) have an important role to play in some churches and the groups responsible for providing these must also be given attention. Many of the good practice points for music listed above can be applied to other groups. However, it is essential that planning and preparation for all creative elements is done as effectively, thoroughly and prayerfully as possible drawing on the expertise of those people who are gifted at initiating such creativity within worship. All groups who offer ministries within worship need to establish themselves within the life of the church so that they meet regularly, pray, practise or plan and enjoy fellowship together.

Good PA system

To have good quality sound you need a good quality PA (public address) system and a trained PA operator. Understandably the budget is often the main concern. If you are in the fortunate position of obtaining good quality sound equipment there are a few pointers to remember:

- An effective music group or band will require good PA resources.
- It's best not to amplify a music group through a PA system designed for spoken word, the sound produced will be poor quality.
- Small, less 'ugly' looking speakers are not necessarily the best.
- The acoustics of every church are different and so each has differing needs with regard to PA.
- Ask for professional advice to help you choose the best equipment for your church with the money you have available.
- When exploring the possibilities of installing a new PA system why not seize the chance to carry out any necessary reordering of space within the church.
- Try to think big. A sufficient PA system today may be inadequate in five years' time.

Note – an organ and choir will almost certainly not require amplification so unless you have an additional music group a PA system for spoken word will suffice.

User-friendly worship

If worship is to be accessible to all, relevant and in touch, then it must be user-friendly. The following can help:

- Ensure that there is only ONE source for all words needed for a service (liturgy, hymns and songs). OHP or data projection are best but service sheets are also effective. (Note – data and overhead projection requires trained operators.)
- A trained welcome team on the door.
- A warm welcome at the start of worship.
- Clear guidelines to inform people of what goes on, where and how (concise).
- Refreshments before or after worship.
- No more than two new songs/hymns in a service.
- Strong, clear worship leading.
- Preaching that is full of life – including the everyday things, life application, stories, humour.
- Contemporary creative elements that link with everyday life.
- Space for people to offer themselves within worship (praise, adoration, thanks, prayers, needs, emotions, etc.)
- No jargon! If 'churchy' terms have to be used then explain their meaning.

Good resources

Good resources are vital to effective ministries. Be on the lookout for useful resources to equip any creative ministries you may have – music, drama, dance and signing. Also keep an eye out for new creative ideas to use – artwork, video material, images, icons, songs, etc.

Planning worship

The planning of worship is an important responsibility and should be undertaken thoroughly and prayerfully. If liturgy is to flow, grow and create space for us to be open to God then we need to provide clear structure and guidance. We also need to be imaginative, open, collaborative and expectant in our approach. The following techniques will help you plan effective worship:

Making appropriate choices

- What type of service is it?
- What is the time scale?
- Who is the service for? (all-age, adult)
- What is the composition of the congregation? (social backgrounds, age)
- Is there a theme?
- What are the readings?
- What liturgy will I use?
- What music is needed?
  Background music
  Instrumental music
  Music to minister
- Where is the music needed?
- Who is playing the music? (e.g. a group, piano only)
- What creative ideas can be included? (artwork, drama, dance, responses, visual elements, etc.)
- Where should I place the creative ideas in the service?
- What is the current church situation? (renewal, building project, growth, conflict, struggling)
- Are there any current prophecies or words of knowledge to be considered?
- What is my prayerful impression of what God might do and what he wants me to do?

When considering the above questions it is important to discuss and prayerfully consider them with those taking part in the service (preacher, worship leader, organist, staff, etc.).

Choosing a worship flow

Worship needs a shape and it must flow so worshippers are led naturally on a journey. This way each aspect of worship will lead on from the last. A worship flow can be built from the following basic outline:

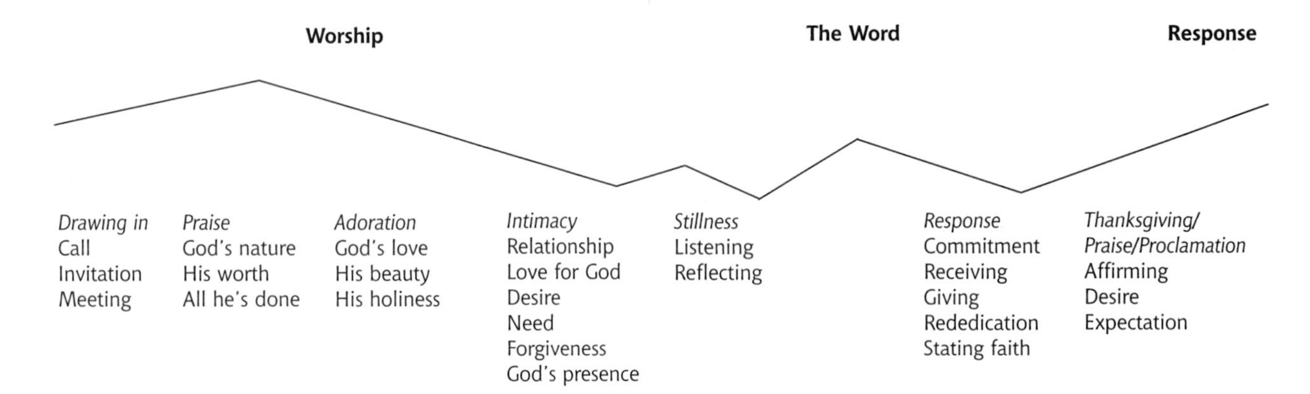

Note – most of the service plans provided are also built on this basic worship flow.

When planning worship we have to decide what aspects will be included and the order in which they will flow within the liturgy or extended time of open worship. A safe principle would be to follow this outline flow and order but with good reason and well-chosen material aspects could be omitted. Any decision would need to take into consideration the theme and other elements of liturgy that need incorporating. The desired worship flow is one that rises and falls naturally at appropriate places as in the example above.

Good examples:
Praise → Adoration → Intimacy → Stillness → Response → Thanksgiving

Drawing in → Praise → Stillness → Praise

Praise → Adoration → Intimacy → Response → Proclamation

The flow to avoid is one that is made up of alternate peaks and troughs.

Poor examples:
Intimacy → Praise → Drawing in → Response

Response → Praise → Thanksgiving → Stillness → Intimacy

Stillness → Praise → Intimacy → Thanksgiving → Adoration → Proclamation

Building creative, God-filled worship on the essential components

The following are the components discussed in 'The essential components of creative Spirit-impacted worship' (page 13). These are the essential ingredients for worship that is contemporary and open to the power of God. Build them into your worship flow and liturgy:

- A desire to see the Spirit of God impacting worship
- Praise
- Adoration
- Intimacy
- Reflection
- Silence
- Response to God's word
- Extended times of open worship
- Intercession
- Prayer ministry
- Freedom of expression
- Creativity

Selecting hymns and songs

A simple principle applies: choose songs that fit with each aspect of your worship flow and liturgy. To do this you will need to have an idea of the main characteristics for each song or hymn; you may find a theme index from a music book helpful.

Example:
If you begin your service with praise then choose songs/hymns to fit this.

Following a time of extended worship you may wish to bring people to a place of intimacy. Therefore make your selection from songs that reflect aspects of intimacy and relationship.

Later in the service you may include a time of response following the sermon/talk. Choose songs appropriate to the response you wish people to make.

Points to remember . . .

- Choose hymns/songs that fit well together (these could then be linked by musicians).
- Avoid using songs at inappropriate places, e.g. songs of intimacy in times of praise or songs of repentance and cleansing after confession.
- Many hymns and songs are versatile and can be used in a variety of places within a worship flow or liturgy because their words cover a lot of ground.
- Only choose songs/hymns that you have the words for.
- Try not to take a theme too literally (e.g. the theme is 'light', choosing songs with the word 'light' in the title).
- Always have a couple of songs up your sleeve just in case (for times of extended worship, prayer ministry, a song that flops).
- Use a good index (e.g. *The Source*).

Leading worship/services

Leading worship is not only a tremendous responsibility but it is also an immense privilege. The leader is not required simply to be the master of ceremonies but to be the facilitator and director of genuine worship that is full of truth and Spirit. Obviously as a service or worship leader you will have been called by God and appointed by the church but you will also need two other attributes – a servant's heart and a willingness to be empowered by God. The following can help with your worship leading:

Worship is a journey

Ensure that it flows and grows.

The importance of welcoming

Warmly welcome the congregation, making visitors feel particularly welcome. Give clear guidelines regarding what will be going on and where things can be found, e.g. 'All the words you will need will be on the OHP'.

Clear guidelines

Be specific in your directions so that people clearly understand what is expected of them or what they are free to do. If you invite 'open' worship where people are free to express spiritual gifts (e.g. prophecy) you may wish to lay down some criteria as a safeguard. Perhaps only invite those who are members of a house group to share.

Demonstrating the value of praise and worship

Ensure that those leading worship or participating in some way are at the front of church when the sung worship begins, otherwise a very clear message will be given out – 'this sung worship is an optional extra' or 'we don't want to be part of the proceedings just yet'.

How you treat hymns and songs also communicates a message. If you have to, try to introduce them well. Encourage all those helping lead the worship (e.g. the music group or band) to look as if they are enjoying themselves. It is essential that you and your colleagues lead by example.

Make the start and the end of a service clear

It is important for people to know what is happening. A clear beginning and conclusion will help set the scene and draw things to a close.

Introducing and directing (liturgy, readings, songs and hymns)

This is very important as it can make or break the flow of worship.

It is best if worship develops in an unbroken flow moving from item to item with very little announcing. For example, instead of announcing a hymn, put the words on the OHP screen. As the music introduction begins people will quickly get the idea that they are about to sing. Similarly, with a reading.

Why not let the reading follow another part of the worship unannounced so that one flows into the other. To do this, leaders of worship, musicians, those reading and praying will need to know what to do and when to do it (see the directions in the Service Outlines provided).

There may be times when announcing or introducing is necessary, i.e. when focusing a time of response, leading into a time of worship or directing how our worship may proceed. Whilst it is important to be clear it is also important to keep it brief and simple.

Concluding times of worship

Often it will be necessary to conclude what has already happened or to summarise parts of worship. Alternatively, you may feel you ought to conclude a time of extended worship with a prayer. Whatever happens, don't preach another sermon. Again keep it simple and brief.

Communication

It is important that during worship you are able to communicate with other leaders of the service (co-worship leaders, music group, preacher). This often happens during open times of worship or times of response. The worship may need to go in a completely different direction and you need to ensure that it does. Inform your colleagues and always encourage them to advise you too.

Sensitivity

It is important that you have your eyes, ears and heart open to be aware of the Holy Spirit and things that God may want to do within worship. If you feel prompted by the Holy Spirit to say something, challenge, encourage or prophesy then act on it.

Before the service pray you will be open to God and lead the worship in his strength.

Open and willing

To allow God to move in power, releasing our hearts in worship and opening our eyes to his will, we have to be open and willing. If we want to be constantly in control then we will greatly limit any time of worship. In short – go with the flow, don't be a control freak!

Facilitate

As a worship leader your role is to help facilitate genuine worship and the free moving of the Holy Spirit. Gentleness, humility and a desire for people to see God, not you, are essential qualities. If you want to be open to new dimensions in worship do it prayerfully with teaching and nurturing. Avoid imposing your own preferences and tastes.

Simplicity

Remember 'simple is best' – don't say too much. Often nothing needs to be said, the silence speaks for itself.

Be yourself, be human

Worship is not a performance and things will often go wrong. Have a sense of humour and remember that both you and the congregation are worshipping together, so enjoy it.

See for yourself

A lot of the ideas and techniques contained in this book may be innovative and new to you. In addition to introducing worship of this nature in your church why not experience similar worship for yourself? Open times of extended sung worship are a main feature of celebrations at events such as Spring Harvest or New Wine. Alternatively, arrange a catalyst event or workshops to help develop the components of creative, God-filled worship in your church.

For further information on creative Spirit-impacted worship events, presentations, training, church worship audits or conferences visit my website:
www.lokate-music.co.uk

Service outlines

A witness to the light

Worship including Communion – ideal during Advent

Order of Service

Directions

A small tea light candle could be placed on every seat or pew, enough for all who will attend. A large unlit candle should be placed on a table visibly at the front of church.

1 ***Welcome and Notices***

Warm and inviting. Visitors and newcomers should be made particularly welcome.

2 ***Introduction to the Theme***

Stand

3 ***Sung Praise and Worship***

Hymn O come, O come Emmanuel (*Sing Glory*)
Song Great is the darkness (*The Source*)

Move directly into praise and worship.

4 ***Open Time***

(Open to God, open prayer or praise, reflecting, sharing gifts)

Play soft instrumental music in background. Open to the Holy Spirit.
The congregation may be encouraged to reflect, pray quietly or out loud. It is important for the worship leader to direct sensitively at this point.

Sit if not already doing so

Soft instrumental music continues in background.

5 ***Time of Confession***

Read 1 John 1:5-7

Reflection

Encourage the congregation to reflect on their need to walk in the light and be purified from all sin. Could conclude time of personal reflection with prayer.

Towards the conclusion of the time of reflection and prayer an extended introduction of the chorus of the song should be played.

Song Great is the darkness (chorus only)

Chorus should be sung slower and quietly to conclude time of confession.
SHORT PAUSE

6 ***The Word***

Reading (John 1:6-8, 19-28)

Atmospheric music plays in background. Photograph slide of 'Daybreak' projected onto screen.

Short Time of Silence

After reading, member of congregation comes forward to light large candle.
SHORT PAUSE
(Projection off. Candle remains lit.)

7 ***Talk***

Talk linked to theme. Challenging and affirming, giving practical help for discipleship.

Silence

For reflection on Talk.

8 ***Response*** – A call to be a witness to the light.

Song The Spirit of the Lord (sung during time of response) (*The Source 2*)

Background music plays softly during introduction to response. Invite the congregation to answer the call to be a witness to the light – Jesus, to commit themselves to sharing the good news in word and action.
People can respond privately in their hearts or can bring out their candle, light it from the large candle and leave it on the table. This will show a personal and collective response by joining each light together. Candles then remain lit as visual focus.

9 ***Informal Peace*** (optional)

The Peace could be shared informally during this time of response. Ideally with people around the table of candles or with nearby people in the seats. If people are unfamiliar with 'the Peace' then explain the meaning (blessing each other with Christ's peace, reconciliation, etc.)

10 ***Prayers***

Music ends.
Prayers continue unannounced.

Let us sit or kneel to pray together:

Come, Lord.
Be our glorious King,
enthroned on the praises of your people.
Establish your kingdom in the hearts of your church
and make us one in you.
Send us out in the power of your Spirit
to live for your praise and glory,
taking your light wherever we go.

Silence

We pray:
come, Lord Jesus.

Come, Lord.
Be our King of kings.
Before you all creation will sing your name,
every knee will bow and every tongue confess
that you are Lord.
May your Lordship be known through all the earth
and may your power be displayed.
We pray for our rulers and governments
and long that they too will acknowledge your authority
over every decision, issue and event.

Silence

We pray:
come, Lord Jesus.

Come, Lord.
Be our servant King.
Just as you sacrificed everything,
may we too give you our all.
Grant us your servant heart
so that we may give of ourselves freely.
Help us to love as you love us
and to reach out
to those who do not know you.

Silence

We pray:
come, Lord Jesus.

Come, Lord.
Be our victorious King.
You have defeated sin and death
and shown your power over sickness and suffering.
In faith we lift to you those who are suffering
through sickness, tragedy or bereavement.
Bring healing where there is none,
hope where there is despair
and life where there is death.

Silence

We pray:
come, Lord Jesus.

Come, Lord.
Be our one true King.
You have shown that there is only one path to walk,
one journey to make and one direction
in which to travel – towards you.
Help all Christian people who profess your gospel
to unite under your gracious power
and join with all the saints to cry . . .

come, Lord Jesus. Amen.

Hymn O for a thousand tongues to sing (*The Source*)

The hymn is announced.

11 *Communion*

A Communion prayer or reading may be said.

Song Great is the darkness (chorus only)

12 *Sharing of Communion*

Songs How deep the Father's love for us (*The Source*)
Such love (*The Source*)
Here is love (*The Source*)

Extended time of worship. Songs linked.

Music ends.

13 *Conclusion*

Prayer, announcements and the offer of prayer with the prayer ministry team.

Hymn Joy to the world (*The Source*) and/or
Song The Grace (*The Source 2*)

14 *Prayer Ministry Available*

Soft worship music could be played as people leave or as prayer continues.

God's gift of grace
Worship including Communion

Order of Service

1 ***Welcome and Notices***

Warm and inviting. Visitors and newcomers should be made particularly welcome.

2 ***Introduction to the Theme***

SHORT PAUSE

Stand

Song Praise the Lord (*The Source 2*) or
Hymn O worship the Lord in the beauty of holiness (*The Source*)

After the song/hymn has been sung, slow the music down and repeat the chorus a couple of times. Softer music then continues in the background.

3 ***Time of Confession***

Read John 3:16-17

Invite those present to ask God for his forgiveness – it is ours because of his wonderful grace.

Stand

Song Thank you for the blood (*WWW 2*)
Hymn Here is love (*The Source*)

4 ***Open Time***

(Open to God, open prayer or praise, reflecting, sharing gifts)

Instrumental music continues gently in the background. Worship leader must be sensitive and go with the flow.

Silence
Sit if not already doing so

Music ends.

5 ***The Word***

Reading (Ephesians 2:1-9)

Short Time of Silence

SHORT PAUSE

6 ***Talk***

Silence

For personal reflection and response to the Talk. How does God want me or us to respond? Maybe guide people's prayers as an opportunity for response.

7 ***Time of Sung Praise and Worship***

Stand initially but people should be free to stand or sit

Songs Thank you for the blood (Reprise)
There's a place where the streets shine (*The Source*)
O Lord, you're beautiful (*The Source*)

Songs linked together with instrumental sections.

8 ***Open Time*** – optional but go with the flow

Gentle music continues in the background.

9 ***Open Prayer***

Sit or kneel if not doing so already

As music continues very softly members of the congregation are encouraged to speak out their prayers or to pray privately. Reassure people that they are not under pressure to pray aloud. Prayer headings could be shown on the OHP as a guide.

The music ends.

10 ***Communion***

A Communion prayer or reading may be used.

11 ***Sharing of Communion***

Songs By his grace (*The Source*)
Thank you for saving me (*The Source*)
Hymn Amazing grace (*The Source*)

Songs and hymn are linked through instrumental music.

Silence

Final hymn is announced.

Hymn Praise, my soul (*The Source*)

Before the Grace offer prayer ministry. Maybe someone wants healing or perhaps something has been highlighted during the worship and they would like to ask for prayer.

Song The Grace (*The Source 2*)

12 ***Prayer Ministry Available***

Soft worship music could continue as people leave or as prayer continues.

Repent, believe and follow

Order of Service

1 ***Welcome and Notices***

2 ***Introduction to the Theme***

Stand

3 ***Sentence of Scripture***

The kingdom of God is near.
Repent and believe the good news! (Mark 1:15)

4 ***Sung Praise and Worship***

Hymn To God be the glory (*The Source*)

Song There is a Redeemer (*The Source*)
Song I will offer up my life (*The Source*)

Silence

5 ***Open Time***

(Open to God, open prayer or praise, reflecting, sharing gifts)

Sit if not already doing so

6 ***Confession***

Hymn Here is love (verse 1) (*The Source*)

(Invite those present to reflect on their need of forgiveness but also on the overwhelming love God has for them.)

Praise be to the God and Father of our Lord Jesus Christ, who has blessed us in the heavenly realms with every Spiritual blessing in Christ. . . . In him we have redemption through his blood, the forgiveness of sins, in accordance with the riches of God's grace that he lavished on us with all wisdom and understanding. (Ephesians 1:3, 7, 8)

Hymn Here is love (verse 2)

Silence

7 ***The Word***

Reading (Mark 1:14-18)

Silence

Directions

Stand a large paper-covered cross clearly at front of church.

Warm and inviting. Visitors and newcomers should be made particularly welcome.

SHORT PAUSE

Read sentence without announcing it.

Introduction to first hymn immediately after Acclamation.

Hymn and songs should be linked with instrumental music.
Soft instrumental music played to conclude opening time of worship.

Open to the Holy Spirit.
The congregation may be encouraged to pray out loud, speak out praise or to share how God has encouraged them. Leader may conclude with an appropriate prayer.

Soft introduction to hymn.

Soft and sensitive instrumental music continues in background to prayer.

Instrumental leads into introduction to verse 2.

Music ends following verse 2.

Photograph slide of footprints in sand or a fishing net and boat projected onto the screen during reading.

8 ***Talk***

Talk linked to theme. Challenging and affirming, giving practical help for discipleship.

Silence

For reflection on Talk.

9 ***Response***

Background music plays softly during introduction to response. Invite the congregation to follow Christ. Perhaps for the first time or in a deeper way. Turning away from old ways or sins, believing with a sincere heart in his forgiveness and all that he offers.

Personal rededication through private prayer

For personal rededication music continues whilst people respond to Christ privately.

or

A practical dedication by placing your own ink thumb-print on the white cross at the front of church.

If members of congregation wish to dedicate themselves to Christ then invite them to respond practically by pledging themselves to the cross of Christ, placing their thumb-print on the white cross at the front of church. This would be their own unique pledge as no one else shares their thumb-print identity. Music moves into song of worship to sing during response.

Song From heaven you came (*The Source*)

SHORT PAUSE

10 ***Prayers***

Move directly into prayers without announcing.

Let us sit or kneel to pray:

Lord, we want to follow you in the way of a servant.
Give us the strength to let go of our selfish desires
as individuals and as a church,
to deny ourselves for the sake of others.
Help us to make it our priority to serve you
by sharing your love in all that we do and say.

Silence

Lord, we'll follow you.
Help us to walk in your footsteps.

Lord, we want to follow you in the way of sacrifice.
May your death on the cross
remind us of all that you gave to bring us forgiveness
and help us to count the cost of truly following you.

Silence

Lord, we'll follow you.
Help us to walk in your footsteps.

Lord, we want to follow you in the way of peace.
We ask that you would give all people
the strength to resist war and hate,
to forgive and live in love.
Through your Spirit help your church
to shine an example of your love
and to embrace the lost,
the despised and those rejected.

Silence

Lord, we'll follow you.
Help us to walk in your footsteps.

Lord, we want to follow you in the way of compassion.
Help us to love as you love us.
May we help you in the work of your kingdom
by bringing comfort to the sick and suffering.
We pray now for those who are suffering at this time
and ask that you will give them the healing touch
of your precious hands.

Silence

Show us how we might help them in practical ways,
giving them friendship and support.

Lord, we'll follow you.
Help us to walk in your footsteps.

Lord, we want to follow you to the gates of glory.
You have walked the path from death into glorious life
and now you lead the way to the place
where we can live with you for ever,
joining with all the saints in your endless praise.

Lord, we'll follow you.
Help us to walk in your footsteps. Amen.

Hymn Be thou my vision (*The Source*)

Announce hymn whilst music intro is played in background.

Before the Grace offer the opportunity for prayer after the service. Maybe people would like to make their pledge on the cross as they felt unable to respond in front of the whole congregation. Perhaps the worship highlighted a need for prayer or advice.

Song The Grace (*The Source 2*)

11 *Prayer Ministry Available*

Soft worship music could be played as people leave and whilst prayer continues.

Palm Sunday – the humble King

Worship including Communion

Preparation

This time of worship could be simple and without trimmings.
It would be most fitting for this service to be conducted in the round where possible. The altar or communion table would be situated in the centre of the congregation and the worship should be led and directed also from within the circle. A table low to the floor could be used for communion and the congregation could also sit on the floor instead of chairs. Cushions could be used and some chairs placed around the outer circle for those who need them. For communion the president could kneel. Members of the congregation could gather and kneel around the table to informally offer one another the bread and wine. Instead of silverware, pottery cups and plates could be used. An unleavened loaf and red wine should make up the meal. For visual inspiration, a bowl or basin and towel could be placed next to the communion table. For easy access to the words of the worship it would be best to use a service sheet. Sung worship and music should be simple and sensitive. Perhaps unaccompanied singing or simple harmony would be appropriate.

Order of Service

1 ***Welcome and Notices***

2 ***Introduction to the Service and Theme***

3 ***Sung Praise and Worship***

Stand

Hymn O Lord my God (*The Source*)
Song I bow my knee before your throne (*The Source*)

4 ***Open Time***

Silence

5 ***Confession***

Humbled before the majesty of the Lord
we see ourselves in a true light.
Give to God the things that burden your heart,
things you should not have done
and things you have failed to do.
Make a new start with the Lord now.

Song We bow down (*The Source 2*)

6 ***The Word***

Reading (Philippians 2:5-11)

Silence

Directions

Warm and inviting. Visitors and newcomers should be made particularly welcome.
SHORT PAUSE

Move directly into praise and worship.

Hymn and song linked together so that worship flow is unbroken.

Open to the Holy Spirit.
The congregation may be encouraged to reflect, pray quietly or out loud. It is important for the worship leader to direct sensitively at this point.

PAUSE

Towards this time of reflection music introduction begins softly.

No announcement of the reading. Should be an unbroken time of listening and reflecting.

7 *Talk*

Talk linked to theme and reading. Informative but also challenging and affirming. Should lead people to point of response or action encouraging them on their journey of discipleship.

Silence
(For reflection and prayerful response)

Worship leader should initiate and guide people's response during silence.

8 *Prayers*

The prayers follow unannounced from the silence.

This first prayer could be prayed corporately or by the worship leader on behalf of the congregation.

If we have any encouragement
from being united with Christ,
if any comfort from his love,
if any fellowship from the Spirit,
if any tenderness or compassion,
then let us be like-minded, having the same love,
being one in Spirit and purpose.
Let us do nothing out of selfish ambition
or vain conceit,
but in humility consider others better than ourselves.
Each of us should look not only to our own interests,
but also to the interests of others.
Our attitude should be the same as that of Christ Jesus.
Grant us, Lord, **your servant heart. Amen.**

Lord, you are in very nature God.
You made yourself nothing
and took the very nature of a servant,
being made in human likeness.
You humbled yourself and became obedient to death –
even death on a cross!
Help all our leaders in government and in the church
to reflect in some small way
the same humility and self-denial.
By putting the lives of others first
and sacrificing their own interests
they will lead by the best of examples and reflect you,
the Servant King who made humility a way of life.

Silence

Grant us, Lord, **your servant heart. Amen.**

Master, God exalted you to the highest place
and gave you the name that is above every name,
that at the name of Jesus every knee should bow,
in heaven and on earth and under the earth,
and every tongue confess that you are Lord,
to the glory of God the Father.

PAUSE

We pray that your name will be exalted in all the earth,
that the people of this nation will know you are Lord,
that this church will be a place
where people meet with you,
and that we will make you visible wherever we go.

Silence

Grant us, Lord, **your servant heart. Amen.**

Jesus, as Lord of all we ask you to be near to those in need
– the sick, the grieving, the lonely and the poor.

Silence

Lord, you have the power to heal and to save
and we ask you to bring healing and wholeness
where there is pain and suffering.
We ask too that you will empower us with your Spirit
and send us out to serve people with your love.

Grant us, Lord, **your servant heart. Amen.**

O God, help us to carry on working out our salvation
with fear and trembling,
for it is you who works in us
to will and to act according to your good purpose.
May we shine like stars in the heavens
as we hold out the word of life
and each day join with all the saints
and all of creation to honour and exalt you.

Grant us, Lord, **your servant heart. Amen.**

Hymn to minister When I survey (*The Source*)

This hymn should be sung for the congregation to help prepare their hearts for communion. Encourage them to meditate on the words.

PAUSE

9 *Communion*

Come, take this bread, this is his body.
Eat and think of him, this is our saving grace.
Take this, his cup, blood shed for many.
Drink and think of him, this is our saving grace.

10 *Sharing of Communion*

Encourage the congregation to approach the table informally, kneel if possible and offer one another communion. Enough cups and plates should be used so that people are not lingering too long. Prayer ministry could be available.

Songs What kind of love is this (*The Source*)
How deep the Father's love for us (*The Source*)
Here is love (*The Source*)

Sung worship should be gentle and sensitive. Perhaps solo singing would be appropriate. Instrumental music linking the songs would be effective and help create an environment of reflection and prayer. Towards the conclusion of communion the music ends.

Silence

Before the final song offer the opportunity for prayer after the service. Perhaps the worship highlighted a need for response, healing or advice.

Song The Grace (*The Source 2*)

11 *Prayer Ministry Available*

Soft worship music could be played as people leave and whilst prayer continues.

Filled with the Spirit

Worship including Communion – ideal for Pentecost

Order of Service	*Directions*
1 ***Welcome and Notices***	Warm and inviting. Visitors and newcomers should be made particularly welcome. SHORT PAUSE
2 ***Introduction to the Theme***	
3 ***Sung Praise and Worship*** (extended time taking in Confession) **Hymn** Holy, holy, holy! (*The Source*) or **Song** Praise God from whom all blessings flow (*The Source*) **Song** As we seek your face (*The Source*)	Move directly into praise and worship.
4 ***Open Time***	Soft instrumental music played in background. Open to the Holy Spirit. The congregation may be encouraged to reflect, pray quietly or out loud and share gifts of the Spirit. It is important for the leader of the worship to direct sensitively at this point. The music then ends softly.
Silence	
5 ***Time for Confession*** *Remain seated*	
Hymn Breathe on me, Breath of God (*The Source*) (verses 1 and 2)	Introduction to the hymn begins unannounced. Instrumental music of the hymn continues softly in the background.
Holy, holy, holy is the Lord Almighty; the whole earth is full of his glory. As we too look upon the Lord we cry with Isaiah, 'Woe to me! I am ruined for I am a person of unclean lips and I live among a people of unclean lips and my eyes have seen the King, the Lord almighty.' Spirit of God we need you to cleanse us, to make clean our lips and sweep away our sin. To breathe new life in us. We lift our eyes to you, Lord, and confess the burden of our hearts.	Encourage the congregation to reflect on our need of the Holy Spirit to cleanse us.
Hymn Breathe on me, Breath of God (verses 3 and 4)	The instrumental music leads into an extended introduction to the hymn. Verses 3 and 4 should build musically to encourage affirmation of forgiveness and new start. SHORT PAUSE
6 ***The Word*** **Reading** (Acts 2:1-21)	Photograph slide or image of a ship's sail or flames could be projected onto screen.

Silence

SHORT PAUSE
(Visual images off)

7 *Talk*

Talk linked to theme. Challenging and affirming, giving practical help for life of discipleship filled with the Holy Spirit.

Silence

For reflection on the Talk. How does God want me or us to respond?

8 *Prayers*

Prayers are unannounced and follow time of silence.

Fill us, Lord – with your Holy Spirit.
May our hearts overflow with thanks,
may our lips sing your praise
and may our lives be renewed with your breath of life.

Silence

We pray:
Holy Spirit, come.

Grant us, Lord – the gifts of your Spirit
that you so desire to pour in us.
Give us the courage and the faith to receive them gladly
and to be released into new depths of life –
life with you.

Silence

Work through our lives and our church in power
so that others may be touched with your love,
and hearts may be won for your kingdom;
all to the glory of your name.

We pray:
Holy Spirit, come.

Awaken us, Lord – to see your purposes and your ways.
Holy Spirit, you are the life-giver
and we love to see you at work within creation
and the world in which we live.
As a nation we are in such need of your power and love.
Breathe new life into the dry bones of faith,
pour living water to quench our thirst for you
and flood this land with hope and healing love.

Silence

We pray:
Holy Spirit, come.

Move, Lord Jesus – within our own community.
Through your saving love reach out to the lost,
the broken and the fallen.
Help us to be your voice calling to those in need
and your hands ministering support and care.
We lift to you now those in need of your healing Spirit
because of sickness and suffering.

Silence

We pray:
Holy Spirit, come.

Thank you, heavenly Father – that through your Son
you have given us the gift of eternal life.
Set this hope in our hearts so that each day
we will live to bring you praise and glory.
Unite your church to be one in heart and mind
so that together we will pray . . .

Holy Spirit, come.

Song O breath of life (*The Source*)

Song begins unannounced. Sing sensitively. Music could continue after whilst people pray or rest quietly.

Music ends.

SHORT PAUSE

9 *Communion*

A Communion prayer or reading may be said.

Before Communion/sharing of bread and wine explain to the congregation that an anointing with oil will be available. Explain that oil is a symbol of the Holy Spirit and by being anointed you are expressing your desire to be filled with the Spirit of God, his life-giving power. People may wish to renew their life with the Lord, may wish to ask for healing or to ask for a specific gift of the Spirit. Whatever the reason, encourage them to go forward to receive Communion and then go to the appropriate area in the church given over for this particular time of ministry.

10 *Sharing of Communion and Anointing with Oil*

Songs/hymns By his grace (*The Source*)
Here is love (*The Source*)
The Spirit of the Lord (*The Source 2*)
Holy Spirit, come (*The Source*)

A trained prayer or ministry team will be needed to administer the oil (a simple sign of the cross on the forehead in the name of the Father, Son and Holy Spirit) and to pray with each person with the laying on of hands.

After the sharing of bread and wine the worship continues as people continue to receive prayer ministry.

Silence

Song There is a Redeemer (*The Source*)

Before the singing of the Grace offer the opportunity for prayer or anointing with oil after the service. Maybe people felt unable to respond earlier but would like to now.

Song The Grace (*The Source 2*)

11 *Prayer Ministry Available*

(Continues as needed)

Soft worship music could be played as people leave and whilst prayer continues.

Worship Jesus first, with everything!

Preparation

The following are the simple guidelines for the visual elements suggested for this worship. To be effective they must be done well and thoroughly. A gifted artist within the church membership could be employed for these tasks. When done imaginatively these visual and experiential aspects of worship can have great impact. However, worship is not dependent on such things and you may wish to keep things simple or to be open and 'go with the flow' of worship on the day.

A large wooden cross could be displayed artistically at the front of church. At the cross, roses should be placed (artificial or real). Baskets of scented rose petals could be placed around the church (with enough petals for each person present). Incense or essential oils could be burned around the church to help create the impression of a fragrant offering to the Lord.

Order of Service	*Directions*
1 ***Welcome and Notices***	Warm and inviting. Visitors should be made particularly welcome.
2 ***Introduction to the Theme***	SHORT PAUSE
3 ***Opening Worship*** *Stand* **Hymn** O worship the King (*The Source*) or **Song** I will praise you (*Release, Global Worship*) **Song** Come, now is the time to worship (*The Source 2*) **Song** Jesus, all for Jesus (*The Source 2*)	Hymn and songs linked together so that the worship flow is unbroken.
4 ***Open Time*** (Open to God, open prayer or praise, reflecting, sharing gifts)	Soft instrumental music continues during open time of worship. As and when appropriate the music ends.
Silence	After the silence the congregation should again be able to pray quietly or out loud, speak out praise or share how God has encouraged them. Leader may conclude this section of worship with a prayer.
5 ***Time of Confession*** **Song** From heaven you came (verses 1, 2 and 3) (*The Source*)	After the open time and silence the introduction to the song begins. Sing verses 1, 2 and 3.
Let us then approach the throne of grace with confidence, so that we may receive mercy and find grace to help us in our time of need. (Hebrews 4:16) We sit or kneel to pray:	Image of cupped hands and water on screen. Soft instrumental music continues in background during time of reflection and prayer. The congregation may be encouraged to reflect on their need of Jesus' forgiveness. Image off. Music moves into introduction for the final verse of the song.
Song From heaven you came (verse 4)	Music ends. Image of cupped hands and water returns to the screen.

6 *The Word*

Reading (Luke 7:36-50)

Silence

Image off.

7 *Talk*

Talk linked to theme and readings. Challenging and affirming, giving teaching on worship and our loving response to Jesus – drawing close enough to kiss (intimacy), kneeling at God's feet (the feet that walked the path to the cross).

Silence

For reflection on the Talk.

8 *Response*

Soft instrumental music of the next song played in background.
Baskets of rose petals to be passed along each row. Congregation are invited to take a petal, hold it in their hands and enjoy its fragrance. They are then invited to look at the cross at the front of church and to consider how they should worship Jesus at this moment. Each can give their fragrant offering to the Lord as a way of giving him everything and drawing close enough to worship at his feet. Then invite them either to sit and give offerings privately in their hearts or to come forward, kneel at the cross and lay their offering there.

Private worship offering (sitting or kneeling)

or

Practical worship offering by kneeling at the cross and placing petal on the cross.

Song I will offer up my life (*The Source*) or
Hymn Come down, O Love Divine (*The Source*)

Music moves into song or hymn to sing during response.

9 *Open Time*

or

Silence

After response instrumental music could continue whilst people pray or express their worship more freely. If you haven't provided a response so far you may feel led to encourage the congregation or to lead them in a heartfelt response. It is important for the leader to be open to the Holy Spirit and to be flexible.

10 *Prayers*

After worship and response, prayers follow on immediately without announcement. Music ends.

You may wish to play in the background a recording of classical or other music suitable to an environment of prayer.

Lord, as we kneel at your feet
receive our heartfelt worship.
May it be a pleasing and fragrant offering only for you.
As sinners we are unfit to draw near
and yet you welcome and embrace us
because your compassion is without end
and you are so eager to forgive.
Our love can never match the love you show
but still we give all we have.
May all our lives be to you
an offering of thanks and praise
so that you alone are glorified above all things.

Silence

Lord, trusting in your love
we give you our prayer.

Lord, we bring before you the world in which we live.
You see the violence, the suffering, the hatred,
the destruction and injustice – your heart must grieve.
As Lord of all we trust that you will continue
to pour your living waters into this thirsty world
so that violence gives way to peace,
suffering turns to healing, destruction gives way to growth
and injustice makes way for truth and fairness.
Grant wisdom and humility to all our leaders
so that strengthened and guided
by your life-changing power
they may work through any situation
in accordance with your will.

Silence

Lord, trusting in your love
we give you our prayer.

Lord, we give to you our own community,
its character, strengths and weaknesses.
We thank you for our homes and neighbours
and ask that you would bless them with your Spirit.
We lift to you the vulnerable members of the community
and ask that empowered by you
we might show them your love and compassion.
May this church be a place of refreshment and refuge
for the weary or the broken
and may we shine as a bright star
leading people to you.

Silence

Lord, trusting in your love
we give you our prayer.

Lord, we bring before you the sick,
the suffering and those in need.
You have power over all things
and we ask you to heal, comfort and provide
for the people we lift to you now . . .

Silence

Lord Jesus, fill us with your compassion
so that we might reach out to those who need us
and spark fresh hope into their lives.

Lord, trusting in your love
we give you our prayer.

Lord, we give you our thanks.
You have shown us such grace and given us true hope.
You are the one true King
who deserves our offerings of worship and love
before and above all things.
Together with all the saints, heavenly hosts
and all of creation
we will proclaim how great you are.

Lord, trusting in your love
we give you our prayer. Amen.

Background music ends.
SHORT PAUSE

Stand

Song My Jesus, my Saviour (*The Source*)

The song starts unannounced.

Before the singing of the Grace offer the further opportunity for prayer after the service. Maybe people would like to make their offering to the Lord at this point as they felt unable to do so earlier. Or perhaps God is encouraging them in some way to respond to what they have heard or sensed in their hearts.

Song The Grace (*The Source 2*)

11 *Prayer Ministry Available*

Gentle worship music could continue as people leave and as prayer continues.

Before the throne of God

Worship including Communion

Order of Service

1 ***Welcome and Notices***

Warm and inviting. Visitors should be made particularly welcome.

SHORT PAUSE

2 ***Sung Praise and Worship***

Stand

Hymn Tell out, my soul (*The Source*) or
Song Let everything that has breath praise the Lord (*The Source 2*)
Song Faithful one (*The Source*)
Song Father, we love you (*The Source*)

3 ***Open Time***

Soft instrumental music played in background.
Open to the Holy Spirit.
The congregation may be encouraged to reflect, pray quietly or out loud and share gifts of the Spirit. It is important for the worship leader to direct sensitively at this point. The music then ends softly.

Silence

After the time of silence you may wish to ask if anyone would like to share some thoughts or testimony with the congregation. Alternatively you may wish to conclude this section with an appropriate prayer.

4 ***Time of Confession***

Read Hebrews 4:14-16

As the Bible passage is read instrumental music to the song 'Before the throne of God above' plays softly in the background and continues through the time of confession.

Time for personal prayer and quiet reflection.

Towards the conclusion of the time of confession the instrumental music leads into an extended introduction to the song 'Before the throne of God above'.

Stand

Song Before the throne of God above (*The Source 2*)

After the song the music ends.

Silence

Sit

5 ***The Word***

Reading (Hebrews 12:1-3)

SHORT PAUSE

Silence

6 *Talk*

Talk linked to theme and readings. Challenging and affirming, giving practical help for discipleship.

Period of Silence and Response

For personal reflection and response to the talk. How does God want each of us to respond? Maybe guide people's prayers as an opportunity for response.

- A song of response could be included here

7 *Visual Prayer*

Using projected headings and images as the guidelines for prayer together with atmospheric background music and spoken introductions to each subject.

Preparation: During the week prior to the service collect newspaper headlines and pictures to use as prayer headings and stimuli. Cut and paste them onto white A4 paper and photocopy onto OHP acetates. Add to this collection other appropriate headings or images you would like to use. These will form the basis for the prayer time. Select some appropriate music to be played in the background. In addition, video material taken from the week's news could be used in conjunction with the OHP.

Explain to the congregation how this form of prayer works – they will see images and headings to guide their prayers, each new subject will be introduced briefly. The congregation could either pray quietly or in small groups.

Background music begins (live or recorded).

8 *Communion*

A prayer or reading.

9 *Sharing of Communion*

Songs How deep the Father's love for us (*The Source*)
Father, you are my portion (*The Source*)
O thou who camest from above (*The Source*)

Songs linked so that the worship flows.

Music ends.

Silence

Stand

Song Salvation belongs to our God (*The Source*)

The song is announced.

10 *Prayer Ministry Available*

Soft worship music could be played as people leave or as prayer continues.

Freedom in worship

Order of Service	*Directions*
1 ***Opening Worship***	Whilst people enter. Sung by music group or band. Includes new songs to be sung during the service.
2 ***Welcome and Notices***	Warm and inviting. Visitors and newcomers should be made particularly welcome.
3 ***Introduction to the Service***	Brief background into the area you hope to explore today. May conclude with a prayer asking God to accomplish his purpose amongst you as you seek him and worship him.
4 ***Sung Praise and Worship*** *Stand* **Songs** Great is the Lord (*The Source*) Lord, I lift your name on high (*The Source*) Father of creation (*The Source*)	Directly into praise and worship after introduction. Three songs should be linked together with instrumental music providing freedom and space for personal expression and openness to the Holy Spirit.
5 ***Open Time***	Open to the Spirit, free worship. Instrumental music continues, worship leader may direct appropriate response – pray quietly, speak out praise, pray out loud.
Silence	Music ends – silence. If not said already, say concluding prayer to Open Time.
Sharing	Give members of congregation opportunity to share a testimony, any words of knowledge, pictures, etc.
Sit if not doing so already 6 ***Time of Confession*** (A reading could be used)	SHORT PAUSE After the pause, begin extended introduction to 'Amazing Grace'.
Reflection	Instrumental music continues gently in background as introduction to confession is said and during time of reflection.
Hymn Amazing Grace (*The Source*)	After reflection, music leads into introduction to hymn. Music builds. Music ends.
7 ***The Word*** **Reading** Luke 7:36-50	SHORT PAUSE
Silence	
8 ***Talk***	Affirming but challenging. Worship at Jesus' feet – preoccupation with Jesus, expression, freedom from restrictions, sacrificial.

9 *Worship and Response*

Songs When the music fades (*The Source*)
Lord, you have my heart (*The Source*)
(more songs may be needed)

Leader should go with the flow in order to guide worship and response. Be open to the Holy Spirit and the way people respond. Musicians be flexible! May include extended instrumentals, open prayer and space to share.
May conclude with prayer said by worship leader. Encourage congregation to seek a new freedom in worship.

10 *Open Time*

Hymn Crown him with many crowns (*The Source*)

Hymn announced.

11 *Conclusion*

Offer prayer ministry. Encourage those who would like to, to stay for prayer or worship. Invite others to leave for refreshments.

12 *Prayer Ministry Available*

Worship music continues softly as people depart and as prayer continues.